July 28/07
love
Michael & Penny
XOXO

for Judy,
useful and beautiful.
—T.M.

Library of Congress Cataloging-in-Publication Data Available

2 4 6 8 10 9 7 5 3 1

Published by Sterling Publishing Co., Inc.
387 Park Avenue South, New York, NY 10016

Text copyright © 2005 by Harriet Ziefert
Illustrations copyright © 2005 by Todd McKie

Distributed in Canada by Sterling Publishing
c/o Canadian Manda Group, 165 Dufferin Street
Toronto, Ontario, Canada M6K 3H6
Distributed in Great Britain by Chrysalis Books Group PLC
The Chrysalis Building, Bramley Road, London W10 6SP, England
Distributed in Australia by Capricorn Link (Australia) Pty. Ltd.
P.O. Box 704, Windsor, NSW 2756, Australia

Printed in China

Sterling ISBN 1-4027-2668-6

For information about custom editions, special sales, premium and
corporate purchases, please contact Sterling Special Sales
Department at 800-805-5489 or specialsales@sterlingpub.com.

# 39 Uses for a WIFE

Harriet Ziefert

drawings by
Todd McKie

Sterling Publishing Co., Inc.

New York

# 1.

doctor

# 2.
## massage therapist

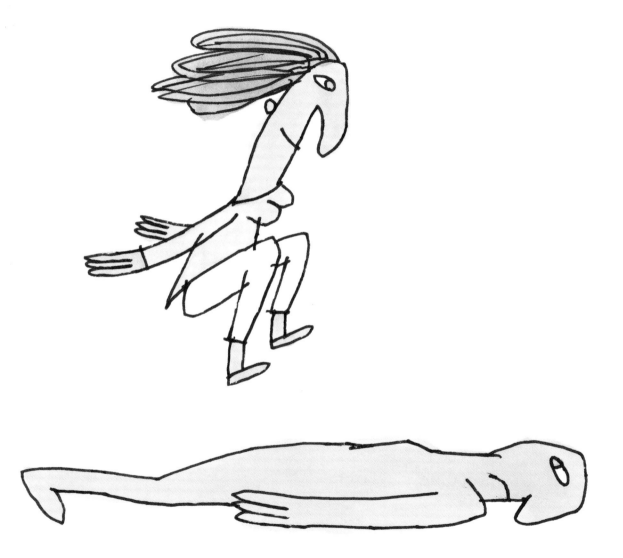

# 3.

# Food processor

# 4.

comedian

# 5.

thermometer

# 6.
## ballast

# 7.

## cleanup committee

# 8.

# bearer of gifts

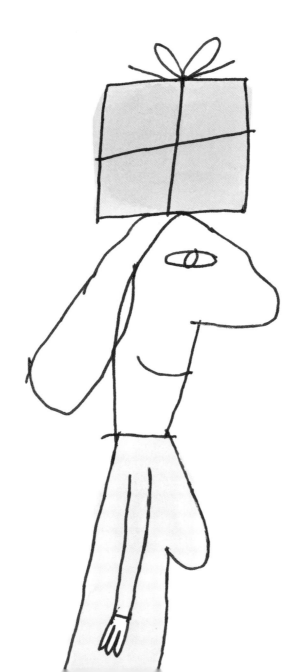

# 9.
# travel pillow

# 10.

## diva

# 11.

## disciplinarian

# 12.
## social secretary

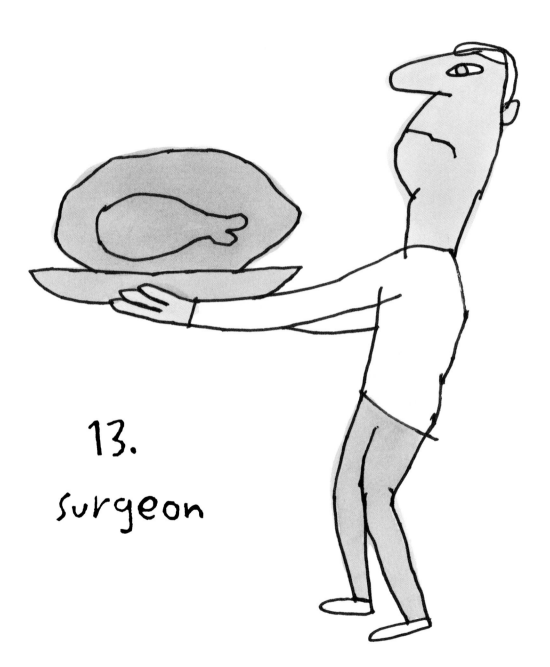

13.

surgeon

# 14.

opponent

# 15.

# Flight attendant – 1st class

# 16.
# lingerie model

# 17.
## chauffeur

18.

dance instructor

# 19.

# audience

# 20. tailor

# 21.
## hair stylist

# 22.

## caterer

# 23.

# farmer

# 24.

## team player

# 25.

## confidante

# 26.
# Florist

# 27.
plaintiff

# 28.
## entertainer

# 29.

# Chief Financial Officer

# 30.
## horticulturist

# 31.
# yoga teacher

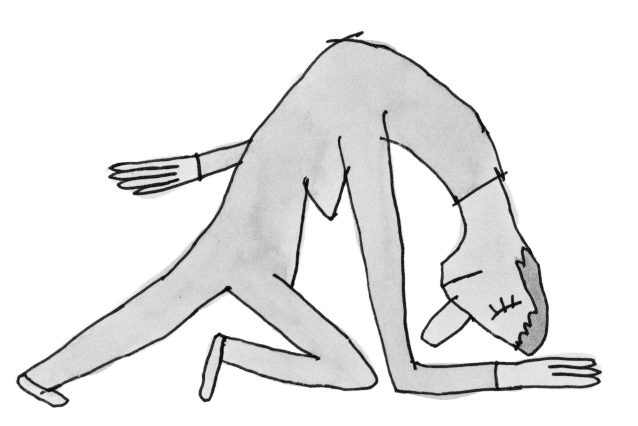

# 32.

# interior designer

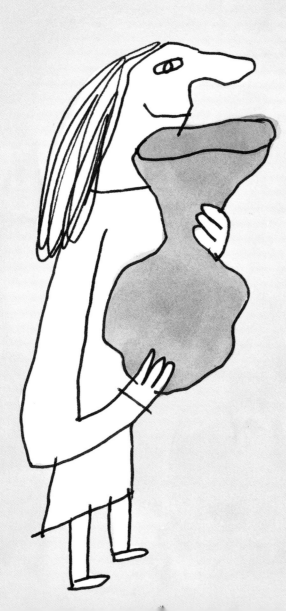

# 33.

# home improvement

# 34.

# trophy

# 35.
## pizza baker

# 36.
## party giver

# 37.
closest friend

38.

hand warmer

# 39.
# Companion